To BARBA

The best

Glenn M Wagner

GREEN GRASS ROMEO

El
Rancho Gumbo

*Five Thousand Days in Montana's
Piegan Country*

Paintings and Stories

by Abner M. Wagner

THE
SAGEBRUSH
PRESS
POST OFFICE BOX 87
MORONGO VALLEY, CALIF. 92256

PRINTED IN THE UNITED STATES OF AMERICA

To my dear wife Ena and our son Kendrick, who never knew El Rancho Gumbo. It was Ena who encouraged me to study writing and art and Ken who expressed his desire to know more about my days in windswept Piegan country.

—A.M.W.

Contents

Foreword

BECAUSE OF ITS profound impact upon my early life, I found myself living the days of El Rancho Gumbo over many times, recounting these stories to my friends and co-workers. I am indebted to them for their interest. Later, questions put to me by our son Ken were the catalyst needed to prompt me in putting the stories into book format. These circumstances, however, should not eclipse the part played by my wife, Ena, who spurred me to study writing and art.

All of the stories and accompanying illustrations are true and I hope that my efforts have filled a few gaps in the history of the West.

I am grateful for the following contributions:

The late Mr. Albert Warner's photo of himself and dredger.

Mrs. Harold (Helen Jane) Johnson and her sister Mrs. Paul (Isabel) Gardner's picture of their father with his one-horse cart.

Other pertinent information by Mrs. Edwina Noffsinger and Mr. Oscar Thronson.

Thanks also to my teachers, Professor Margaret Walters of the University of Washington; Zola Helen Ross, well-known author of Northwest historical novels, co-founder of the Pacific Northwest Writer's Conference; and Mary Ellen Clark, popular local artist and Community College instructor.

Photos of paintings are by Marchand Studio, Everett, Washington.

—THE AUTHOR

El Rancho Gumbo

CHAPTER 1

El Rancho Gumbo

AN EAST-WEST section line bisects the town of East Glacier, Montana. Thirty-six miles east, on that section line, one finds the site of what was then El Rancho Gumbo. Its 320-acres was the allotment of No Bear, a patented Indian. After his death it was advertised for sale. In 1921, my father purchased the allotment for the sum of $1600.00. The patent deed was signed by President Calvin Coolidge.

The land was raw prairie, covered with a fine stand of Buffalo Grass. We moved on in 1923. The first abode was a tent, then a 12 x 16 foot one room shack was erected. Lodgepole Pine for fence posts and a corral were hauled from the Heart Butte area. Logs for a house were shipped from west of the mountains in 1924. Construction was begun in 1926 but the house was not ready for occupancy until 1928. About 1930, my brother purchased a set of logs from a neighbor who had decided to not build a house after all. They were excellent logs, better than the house set and he erected four walls on a good concrete foundation, but the barn was never completed. During the years, a stable, hen house, hog house, and granary were erected. I later covered the log barn with a pole and straw roof and converted the hog house to a cow barn.

A well drilled in 1926 had plenty of clear, cold water,

loaded with Epsom and Glauber's salts and table salt. It was usable with plenty of pumping out but was extremely hard and slimy tasting. It took getting used to, being a real purgative to the uninitiated. Rain and snow water were collected to supplement it for washing purposes. Livestock loved it.

Each log of the house at El Rancho Gumbo was scribed and grooved to fit over the one below it, then caulked with flax fiber and tarred oakum. The house was firred and its four rooms sealed with sheetrock. The kitchen and living room were floored with eight foot lengths of clear and birds eye hard maple which cost $70.00 per thousand feet. We spent many days and evenings on our knees, drilling holes with a Yankee drill to lay the flooring. The two bedrooms and attic were floored with four-inch vertical grain fir. The hard maple was also used on cabinet tops and a five-foot gate leg table was made from it. My brother had tools and was an excellent cabinet maker, doing all of this work. He also made a pair of swinging French doors between the kitchen and living room. A basement excavation was started but never finished due to lack of funds. The roof was the very best grade of cedar shingles. The house was wired for electricity, which never arrived and a bathroom space became a closet for lack of plumbing, which also never materialized. It was a good house, solid in the wind and warm when a fire was kept. I have wished many times that I had that house here (in Everett, Washington) as my home.

I do not have any record of the total cost of the house but do recall that the order of house logs did not fill the railroad car and it was filled out with corral poles. The logs cost $1.00 each and the poles cost $0.25 apiece for a total of $100.00 plus the freight which came to $60.00 laid down in Valier, I believe. I am not quite sure about the freight but do remember the log costs clearly.

I resided at El Rancho Gumbo from 1923 to 1936. During that time mother died, my brother married and left the state, and Dad was transferred from the Blackfeet Irrigation Project to other projects, some out of state, and I remained as the lone resident and operator. No other relatives, close or distant, were in the area. My father, holding the position of Watermaster on the Badger-Fisher Division of the Blackfeet Project, had purchased the land so that he might have his home where his job was. He never intended to engage in ranching but wished it to be for the rest of the family while he continued to hold his position.

There were several reasons for my departure in the end. High on the list was the miserable loneliness resulting from changes in the family and neighborhood. It wasn't worth it. The area had never been blessed with an oversupply of young women of my age bracket and most of them took off for business college or parts unknown, scattering to Great Falls, Havre, and Spokane, as they had no intention of struggling through the gumbo muck all summer to be frozen like popsicles the following winter, and I had no desire to spend my life alone.

HORSE COUNTRY

CHAPTER 2

Horse Country

DURING OUR FIRST years on El Rancho Gumbo there were horses everywhere, hundreds of them, from cayuse runts to 1600 pound outlaws. Many years before, the U.S. Government, good Samaritan that it was, wanted to make farmers out of the Indians and placed draft stallions on the reservation to upgrade the stock. But the Piegans were buffalo hunters, not farmers, and were not about to hand pamper and baby-sit any horse too big to ride. They turned the stallions loose to roam the grassy plains and breed their cayuse mares, raising hordes of big range-bred baddies. Many lovers of horse flesh today would have marveled at the sight of those droves of beauties mirroring their ancestry in the Perche or Devonshire. Diamonds in the rough with knotted manes and tails, they were snow white, coal black or dappled in between; blood bay, steel dust, sorrel and palomino too. Whatever the color, the fact remained, many were mankillers and tough to handle. Every bunch had a stallion who was dangerous and would attack a rider.

El Rancho Gumbo was detached, by a couple of miles, from the lower part of the project which was being farmed for wheat. Three strands of barbed wire were all that separated it from the open range. Keeping ahead of the roving bands was a full-time job. We used to go out and chase them away from our fence because the big ones kicked the little ones through it and trampled our crop. Having no radio or T.V. then, chasing *knotheads,* as they were commonly call-ed, was as good as any pastime. One of the few diversions indulged in by ranchers of the area was corraling a bunch just to look them over and read the brands.

Notwithstanding the freedom of the open range, the cayuse's life was not an easy one, through fly time of sum-mer to the deadly blizzards and bitter cold of winter. To one not familiar with that way of life, some of the condi-tions which existed and happenings which occurred would be unbelievable. Mares usually foaled in the spring or early summer but a birth could take place any time. I have gone out to haze a bunch away and found among them a newly born foal, still wet and the mother not cleaned. It was im-possible to cut them out so they could be left behind and at the same time the others had to be removed from our field or we would be out of the grain business, pronto. There was only one thing to do, whoop it up and start them on their way, mother included with the little guy out in front, run-ning as fast as his little legs could carry him. His lot was not blessed with the brightest of futures either. The stallions were miserable incestuous egotists, always angry and deter-mined to eliminate all unwanted competition for the mare's affection. If one was in a particularly bad mood he might, in jealous rage, grab the foal's neck in his powerful jaws and snap it then and there. There was nothing the poor mare could do about it. At any rate, stud horses spent most of their time fighting each other or biting and kicking the mares in the belly for the slightest infractions of their code or simply for recreation. It was nothing short of miraculous that any colts went full term or survived at all.

El Rancho Gumbo lay on a rolling slope which bottomed out on Fisher Flats. North of the middle of the ranch there was the east end of a high ridge. This ridge connected with a range of hills which circled west and south to connect with another east-west ridge. The basin within this cirque was about three miles by five miles in size. The flat bottom graduated from good buffalo grass land to blue gumbo at its center where a large alkali lake was contained in it after the spring run-off or was fed from wasted irrigation water. In dry years the lake was gone by midsummer. From its position on the slope El Rancho Gumbo commanded an excellent view of the basin. During the peak horse years it was possible to stand in the ranch yard and observe more than a thousand range horses grazing or moving in bands numbering from a few head to two or three hundred. When a bunch approached our fence, one of us would saddle up and ride out to start them moving west into the hills. As soon as they began to move, the others took up the cue and in less time than it takes to tell it the whole alkali flat would be shrouded in a huge cloud of dust as the entire mass of range horses galloped westward. It was, however, a tremendous exercise in futility for they almost always beat the wrangler home again.

While selective breeding was out the window, raising horses was no problem at all. Most of the ranch mares at that time pioneered the art of getting pregnant without benefit of license and we ended up with more colts by accident than most eastern breeders could ever hope for by planned management. And because most of the affairs were clandestine there was no way anyone could make a paternity claim, but we never knew what we were getting until the colt stood and sucked or later came to maturity. These "accidentals" from our mares were sold to buyers who shipped from coast to coast. A substantial number never caught the train out due to reasons best left unmentioned. The biggest horse markets at that time were in up-state New York; Montreal, Canada; Harrisburg, Pennsylvania; Grand Island, Nebraska; Snohomish, Washington; San Francisco, California; and Honolulu, Hawaii.

Recently unearthed from a storage of old treasures in our home, a book published by the Department of Resources, State of Montana, reveals statistics long forgotten. Its cover is missing along with several pages and I can find no date, but it is broken down by counties and is filled with a wealth of information. From this book I have recovered a figure, now hard to believe, even by one who witnessed the era. Their records show that there was, in the year of 1926, a population of 576,000 horses and 11,000 mules in the state. At that time Montana was blessed with approximately 600,000 people. This meant that there was a horse or mule for almost every man, woman, and child, babies included.

My Mother, 'Deelie Wagner,
on Buck about 1910

Mother had a health problem for several years before coming to the ranch. Doctors in Spokane and Montana failed to understand it at first. In February, 1926, she became ill and a nurse was procured to attend her at the ranch, in the shack. We men slept in the garage. April found her in the hospital at Conrad, Montana, where she remained—except for one week back home—until she passed away September 3rd at age 48. Her trouble was then diagnosed as cirrhosis of the liver. It was not from alcohol, as both she and Dad were strict abstainers.

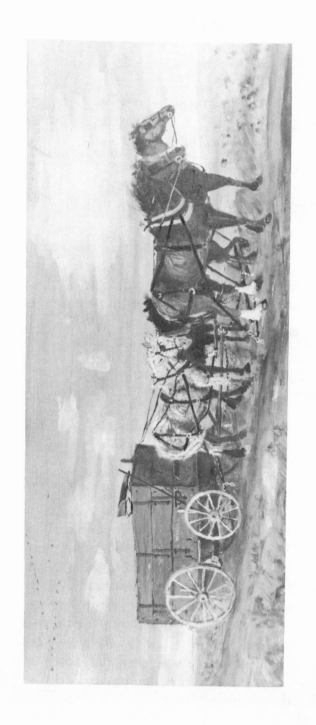

Ten Minute Break

CHAPTER 3

Ten Minute Break

WHEAT HAULING BEGAN after harvest and continued all through the winter. Very little grain was harvested before September and some threshing was done as late as November. The wheat was put directly into granaries at the ranch and later hauled to town after threshing was completed. Before trucks came into general use, all of the hauling was done with horses and wagons. Grain wagons with boxes, three side boards high, held 100 bushels, and wagons with high, flared boxes, called grain tanks, held 150 bushels. With wheat weighing sixty pounds per bushel, these loads were three tons and four and one-half tons. Wagons with high wheels were used, as they were easier to pull than the low wheeled ones. Four big horses were required to pull a regular wagon or a grain tank, but sometimes a trailer wagon was pulled and that took six head to do the job.

There were no paved roads. Until the late twenties they were not even graded; just trails meandering across the prairies or between the fences of a right of way following the section lines. If it ever rained, God help the hauler! Much of north central Montana is gumbo, and if the loaded wagons did not bog down and get stuck, the wheels picked up tons of gooey adhesive gumbo until they became so lumpy or jammed against the brake shoes that they had to be cleaned with a stick or shovel. Sometimes the sticky mud could only be removed by hand. Hauling in freezing weather was never a picnic but the going was easier on frozen roads. Wet roads often did not dry quickly and although they appeared dry on the surface, were soft and spongy for a loaded wagon. The horses were shod in the winter time for traction on icy roads. This presented another problem, to the rancher's feet, for the horse's shoes were fitted with sharp calks which were rough on toes that got stepped on. Some ranchers had bob sleds which would hold a wagon box or a tank. These were better than a wagon if there was enough packed snow, but the big problem which limited their use was the eternal wind. These Infernal Winds, as we called them, blew out of the Rockies and raked the prairies almost every day from late October until the first of May, sometimes attaining incredible velocities. I have been bowled over more than once and blown from a horse by one of those blasts, but never knew just how hard they were until many years after I had left El Rancho Gumbo and was doing survey work for the U.S. Army Corps of Engineers. Working the Pine Tree Line of radar sites, where accurate weather stations were maintained, I found the one at Cottonwood, north of Havre, logging gusts well over 100 miles per hour. Cold winds drifted the dry snow piling it in the roadways behind fences loaded with Russian Thistle tumbleweeds, creating gigantic drifts difficult to get any vehicle through, or clearing other stretches of road, making them impassable by sled. At other times the chinooks came, moderating the temperature 50° or more, melting the snow and leaving anyone caught out with a sled stranded in a sea of mud amid rivulets running every way imaginable.

The story often told was Welker's run from Dupuyer

to Valier. Ed carried the mail between Valier and Dupuyer
which was sixteen miles west. He had just left the town
limits of Dupuyer, driving a team on a sled when a westerly
chinook slammed into the rear of his outfit. Standing in
his sled, he began yelling and lashing the horses' rumps, urging them ahead as fast as they could gallop. All the way to
Valier he lashed and shouted as the horses gave their all, his
sled with its front runners on the snow and the rear ones in
the mud. And just as Ed pulled up in front of the Valier
post office, the last tiny bit of snow melted and ran down
the gutter.

El Rancho Gumbo was 18 miles from Valier and 20
from Cut Bank. Either way the wheat was hauled, it was
more than an eight hour drag, requiring an overnight stop
in town. It was pretty cold duty on some of those hauls
when the bottom dropped out of the thermometer. It was
especially rough when we were breaking in a new horse or
two. This was a job we liked to do in the winter when a
green bronc could be put in the wheel team of a heavily
loaded wagon in deep snow where he could not jump around
too much. It was safer here than trying to break one on a
field job where he would be hitched to a tillage machine.
The one bad part of this deal was that the driver had to stay
up on the wagon seat and hold onto the two pairs of lines
used to drive the strung out teams. If a man had a four-up
of old standbys he could hang the lines on the stake or somewhere on the side of the wagon and walk behind in the
broken trail to keep warm. But with a green one in the
string, it was hang on tight, all the way, and this was hard
to do walking beside the wagon in the deep snow.

I recall one day when both of us were hauling. My
brother had 160 bushels on two wagons with six-up and I
had a four-up on one wagon with a knothead on the wheel

(wheel team). We used to purchase World War One ambulance driver's mittens from a mail order surplus house in Kansas. These were one-finger type, that is besides the thumb, there was a separate index finger, leaving just three in the mitt part. These were good to drive teams with two sets of lines because the wheel team lines were held between the index and third finger. The thermometer was hovering around 28° below zero and my feet became so cold they were numb. After we had dumped our loads at the grain elevator and put the horses in the livery barn for the night, I jumped into a tubful of steaming hot water at the Valier Hotel to get warm. This turned out to be the worst thing I could have done because my feet began to sting and tingle and were sore and painful for a long time afterward. For years following that incident I suffered with an aggravating case of chilblain. I have heard and also read a lot of arguments about how to thaw a frozen person. Some say use cold water or snow, others say use hot packs, but all I know is that never again would I do what I did that night.

We did not have running water or a bath tub at the ranch but only the old Monarch range, with its reservoir, and a wash tub to use on Saturday night, so whenever we got close to a real bath tub with plenty of hot water it was too good to pass up. I don't remember how many rooms the Valier Hotel had and can remember only one bathroom. If that was it I think probably everyone in the west end of Montana had been in it at one time or another. The rooms had large china pitchers and bowls on a stand.

Cut Bank, the county seat of Glacier County, located on the main line of the Great Northern Railroad (now Burlington Northern), was a larger town than Valier, but its livery facility was less pretentious. Its one huge horse hotel, beside the railroad track at the east end of town, was operated by the Miller sisters, two aged and austere ladies. Times were not the best and they managed the barn as frugally as they lived, taking the wheelbarrow up the track to a grain elevator which dispensed hay, to get a bale or two only if equine guests arrived for the night. The barn was not wired and when we pulled in after dark, they lighted our way with a kerosene parlor lamp. This lamp was a thing of beauty, one of those treasures, now antique, having a large china bowl decorated with a profusion of colorfully painted flowers around the chimney. Holding the lamp high, one of the sisters would move from team to team until we had watered, unharnessed and fed all ten horses. I will always remember them as two of the most unforgettable—may they rest in peace—for they did not burn the barn down with all of us in it.

A typical expense for overnight was:

Livery stable, 10 horses @ $ .50	$ 5.00
Room for two, Cut Bank or Valier Hotel . .	1.50
Dinner for two @ $ .65	1.30
Breakfast for two @ $ .35	.70
TOTAL:	$ 8.50

The First House

WAGNER 83

CHAPTER 4

The First House

WHEN THE RANCH was purchased it was raw prairie with nothing on it. The first abode was an 8 x 10 foot wall tent pitched near the northeast corner of the land. Within a month a 12 x 16 foot one-room shack was erected. This would be a temporary living quarters until a better house could be built. It had a single layer bent board box car roof covered with tar paper. The walls were drop siding over shiplap, with brown building paper between, on the outside of the studdings. There was no inner wall, the studs being exposed to the room. Three of the walls had one sliding barn window sash each, and a door was hung in the middle of the building's east end. A single layer of six-inch width fir flooring was layed, that is there was no sub floor. The building was erected on log skids. Not long after its completion, the shack was dragged to a ridge near the center of the land and that location became the permanent homesite of the ranch.

The east end of the shack became the kitchen. A used Majestic range with hot water reservoir and wood box was installed in the southeast corner. The stove pipe, connected directly to a galvanized roof jack, had an asbestos collar to keep the roof boards from catching fire. There were windy days when the stove top and stack were red all the way. Just why the shack never burned to the ground will never be known. North of the door, a board cupboard with upper and lower gingham curtains strung on wires held all of the dishes and most of the packaged food. Between the cupboard and the door, the shelf holding the water bucket and wash basin was also curtained below to hide the waste water bucket, traditionally known as the "slop bucket".

The middle of the shack must have been the dining room because that is where the one and only table was. Farther back, about two and one-half feet, were the bedrooms; two beds separated from the living area and from each other by longer curtains, also strung on wires. What might be referred to as the clothes closets were large spikes driven into the studdings, to be used as hooks to hang things on. Above these, storage shelves held everything that could not be jammed under the beds. My brother and I had grown up in five and ten room modern and semi-modern houses so this was found to be a mighty compacted type of living. For a long time, during the construction days of the Blackfeet project, Dad had lived most of each year in camp shacks and was used to it, probably never realizing what it was like to the rest of the family.

While Mother was with us, the floors were scrubbed religiously and all of the curtains were kept neatly washed and ironed, but after she died I won't say how often such maintenance took place.

Our baptism by wind came in the late autumn when the winds, presaging a change of weather, began gusting to incredible velocities, until one, a little harder than the preceeding gusts, picked up the west end of our shack and let it drop again while we were in bed at night. We had already experienced considerable shaking of our abode on several occasions, and when this one hit, that was all it took. Mother

flew out of bed, and urging us boys to accompany her, headed for the root cellar close by, where we spent the balance
of the night. Dad, however, refused to move, stating flatly
that he had witnessed these winds before, while living in
shacks, and hadn't blown away yet. The wind subsided by
daybreak and we resumed life as usual to await and prepare
for a coming snow storm. However, Mother demanded that
the shack be anchored, so we brought up two short corral
poles about ten feet in length and placed them as props at
the east end of the building. Later, the wind tried skidding
the back end over, so we fastened poles on the roof to dead-
men anchored behind the shack by cables. Now there was
no way anything short of a dynamite blast could move the
shack.

It was a great life. Many of the local ranchers were living on leased Indian lands, owning none themselves, so a
great variety of housing was scattered about the flats. Some
lived in wagon houses with the wheels off, others in all kinds
of combinations of unused granaries set together, and a few
in poorly built two or three-room houses. I think there was
one good five-room house in the neighborhood which was
ten miles away.

Local mines along the bluffs of Birch Creek produced a
low grade lignite coal. Every year several tons were hauled
to the ranch for winter heating and cooking. It took a lot
of kindling, a scarce item, to ignite this coal, and the lignite
was very hard on stove grates because large chunks of slate
would get stuck in them, and we broke more than one grate
getting it out. During the winter months, when we had the
snow barrel in the shack for water, it took plenty of stoking
the old Majestic with coal to keep the temperature livable.
Blizzards howled through the cracks which we stuffed with
papers and rags and the building paper buzzed between the

boards. Many times we wore our heavy coats in the house
and stayed close to the stove. Winter was always two-shirt
weather during the cold snaps. The shack had been banked
up enough to cover the log skids and seal the building underneath, but one winter it got so cold we resorted to banking it more with barnyard manure. The ground was frozen
solid to a depth of several feet, making it impossible to get
more earth fill. I would not recommend this today for,
admittedly, the atmosphere within the shack was not of
quality found in modern houses of today, but because the
manure was quickly frozen and remained so until spring,
it was not all that bad either. This held the essence of horse
to a minimum and it merely served to modify the pervasive
odor of distillate tractor fuel with which most of our cloth-
ing, and our bodies, were saturated. The emergency banking
was removed after the spring thaw and good dirt installed
in its place. The scratchy, part-wool long johns were also removed at this time of year. Boy, what a relief!

During the coldest winter months we removed only our
boots and trousers at bed time, leaving our heavy shirts and
socks on at all times. Double cotton blankets were used instead of sheets, and besides two or three heavy soogans
(comforters) we piled on all the sheepskin coats and mack-
inaws available. Underneath the mattress, several layers of
newspapers covered the springs to hold out the cold from
underneath and there usually were a couple of soogans under the blanket that was slept on. This won't sound so
ridiculous when I tell you that the lowest temperature recorded while we occupied the shack was 60° below zero,
and on a number of other occasions the mercury ranged
from 45 to 58° below. With skimpy baths in the wash tub
occurring only once a week at best, it probably was good
that we were deodorized with the fragrance of Eau de
Horse *à la* Distillate.

My first winter at El Rancho Gumbo was punctuated

by a stay at Mrs. Angel's rooming house in Valier. Here at the Montana House I batched in a back room, near the sink in the hallway. The room had a two-burner kerosene cook stove and a single cot. This arrangement was so I could attend high school. However, it was interrupted at Christmas time because there had been insufficient income from the ranch the first summer, and Dad's wages which were staking the operation did not stretch far enough to maintain my residency away from home. Therefore I became a jerk-out and the resumption of my education is another story.

The fruit acreage in the Spokane Valley, which had been our home before we moved to El Rancho Gumbo, was sold and Mother stored the furniture. Later, when logs were hauled to the ranch for construction of the new house, we erected a one-car garage, before the house was started, and the furniture was shipped over. That winter, after Mother died, my brother was at the irrigation camp helping Walter True repair equipment. That left Dad and me alone at the ranch. During the winters he conducted most of his project duties from the ranch as it was mostly paper work, and his "office" at the camp was a thin walled wagon house set on blocks and too cold to work in. He continued to sleep in the shack and I set up a bed and the German heater, a large cast iron heating stove, in the garage. However, few fires were built there as I would run out at bed time and crawl under a mountain of soogans. The thermometer hit 58° below zero that winter but I was quite comfy. My biggest problem were the doors which swung outward at the east end of the building. The wind at night would pile snow against them and Dad had to dig me out in the morning.

Mother did not live to see the completion of the new house, and when it was finally ready, three bachelors moved in. It was a much improved residence which no longer required that we sleep with our socks on. That alone was priceless.

SPACE FLIGHT

CHAPTER 5

Space Flight

ZAMBEEZIE WAS A black grey with a skunk mane and tail. When you looked at him across the corral he was a shiny black but when you got up close he wasn't that way at all. Instead, he was almost as white as he was black and his tail and mane were half and half. I'd guess that he just had to be born that way because it wasn't the only way he fooled you.

Zam was a ridgeling, which means that he came into this world with a birth defect a little hard to explain to an urban society sprinkled with fair young ladies. The truth was he adored the fillies but he could never be a papa. And for that reason he was so ornery that we never could get together without first having a tall argument about who was going to be the boss that day. It usually took about 45 miles to get his steam gauge down from the red mark and if he ever got a little bit of oats stuck between his ribs it would take another 10 or 15 to do the trick.

This particular day was such a scorcher I could have fried a dozen eggs on the heat waves bouncing back up from the flats. Four a.m. was 40 miles behind and I had had about all of the alkali dust and swarming vermin I could take for one day, when this whopping big horse fly bit old Zambeezie right square in the caboose and he busted in two, leaving me sitting way up there in the middle of the sunburnt sky. By the time I got back to earth he was already half way home and I had nothing but a big sore spot and a ticket on foot for the three miles between me and El Rancho Gumbo.

When I arrived at the south gate, Zam was there waiting for me to open it so he could get in. This I did, but not before informing him, with the toe of my boot, what I thought of him. To get even with him I cancelled all of his dates for the next two weeks, but it didn't do any good. I might as well had pneumonia.

WALTER TRUE, J. G. WAGNER's head ditchrider on the Fisher Flats division, Blackfeet Indian Irrigation Project, pictured above, circa 1925. These ditchrider's carts were used until 1933. The horse was owned by Mr. True. The Project owned a number of mules in previous times and one or two were still used on the carts. A ditchrider carried a shovel and fencing tools to let himself through where gates did not exist or to repair gates that were in bad shape. He also carried a water delivery record book and weir tables to be used when measuring deliveries. Other items included his lunch and a rain slicker.

[33]

DITCHRIDER

CHAPTER 6

Ditchrider

DITCHRIDERS ARE IMPORTANT members of an irrigation project's personnel. In the earlier years theirs was a new job requiring the ability to develop skill in handling and measuring flowing water. On Federal and Carey Act projects it was a good job which included repairs and maintenance duties outside the water delivery season. A few concrete structures were erected but most of the weir boxes, checks and lateral gates were of timber, frequently needing repair or replacement. The ditchrider with a year-long job had plenty to do, work calling for rough bridge type carpentry. Excavation for these features was by fresno, drawn by rancher's horses or government mules. A lot of back busting labor sometimes occurred on the end of a fresno handle. Often more brawn than brains was required to skin a four-up of husky farm chunks (chunky work horses) while loading and dumping a half-yard scraper. Later, when more modern machinery showed up, some ditchriders became operators of Ruth dredgers and bulldozers. On the Federal projects the position eventually became listed on the Civil Service register.

Water delivery in a settled area was pleasant work where one was in contact with ranchers most of the day, but a feeder canal patrolman's job was a much different story.

The long canals running from a source of supply to a storage reservoir or from the reservoir to a farmed area sometimes wound for miles through lonely open range country where one was lucky to see one cowhand or sheepherder or maybe none at all during his entire day of work. Not only was it a lonely drag, but severe weather often brought hair raising moments when the rider was caught in a violent hailstorm, miles from a shelter of any kind. I recall being in just such a predicament when I frantically filled my sombrero with grass for padding against the bullets from heaven. Sometimes the horse was not the most reasonable guy to get along with at such a time. I have seen horses so charged with static electricity during impending storms that their tail hair stood out at right angle to the bone and sparks bounced off the tips of their ears. Under these conditions the job wasn't much better than cowpunching in the old days, about the only difference being that the Gopherpuncher (ditchrider) made it all the way back to his own bunk at night instead of sleeping under the stars with tarantulas and rattlesnakes for bed partners.

There were no rattlesnakes in this part of the country and gophers abounded in droves. These small buckskin colored animals, belonging to the ground squirrel family, continually wreaked havoc with both crops and ditchbanks. They were constantly burrowing into the latter, sometimes going too far and starting a leak. The soils varied from light clay to gumbo, both of which eroded easily. This is why a daily inspection of every foot of a canal was required. Given time, a large section of canal bank could wash out and it would take several days before costly repairs could be completed, days that were critical to the rancher whose crop was thirsty. The canal rider carried a shovel and when a gopher hole was noted, immediately filled it in. If he could find a sizeable rock it was placed firmly over the backfill. These animals were such an agricultural nuisance that the Extension Service waged a vigorous campaign against them by supplying the ranchers with poisoned oats to be placed in spoonfuls down each burrow. While the program had its benefits, too often pest control measures backfired and this was no exception. More than one valuable horse or cow was lost to the poisoned grain.

In the beginning all federal projects were constructed on Indian lands, probably because it was a new experience and the Indian lands were under wardship of the government. The agency involved in the first developments was known as the United States Reclamation Service (USRS), now designated the Bureau of Reclamation. In 1924 all projects on Indian reservations were separated from that department and placed under the direction of the Indian Service with the title United States Indian Irrigation Service.

YELLOW KIDNEY

CHAPTER 7

Yellow Kidney

THE GRAIN WAS CUT with a horse-drawn binder and the bundles stood up in shock rows in the field where they were to sweat for several weeks. When it was ready, the threshing machine was pulled into the field and belted to the tractor which would run it. A wagon was pulled alongside the thresher to receive the grain. The bundles were then hauled to the thresher in open sided racks. Our machine would handle the input from four bundle rack wagons hauling steady.

Some men would follow the harvests across the country. Indian men from other parts of the reservation came to work in our harvests on Fisher Flats. Yellow Kidney was an old man when he came down from Heart Butte to haul bundles for us at threshing time. Tall and willowy, he was an aristocrat of the old school, clad in the finest squaw chewed buckskin suit to be had anywhere. His shiny black hair, with only a few greys showing, hung in neat braids from a cranium filled with the wisdom of the great eagle and the wild dog that howls. This he demonstrated daily by such acts as simply unbuckling the harness and leading the horses out of it, leaving it hitched to the wagon. Yellow Kidney was pragmatic to the nth degree, casting aside all items he figured were unnecessary to accomplish his job. At the dinner table he layed aside the whiteman's tools, preferring to use the long bony ones the good Lord had equipped him with. In the field he worked at a slow but steady pace, pausing only for an occasional swig from the canvas water bag or to roll a Bull Durham cigarette.

The bundle wagons were made for easy loading with a three-tined pitchfork. The racks were constructed with high slatted ends stayed by diagonal braces at the sides. Thus most of each side was left open for loading the bundles in alternate layers of butt-in and butt-out, to form the containment walls of the load. When the wagon was loaded, the hauler would climb up the front of the rack to get aboard for the trip to the threshing machine. But not Yellow Kidney. He had his own way of doing things. And others on the crew never ceased to be amazed, for instead of going up the way the other drivers did, he simply shinnied up the side of the load where only the ends of the grain bundles protruded. We never figured it out; maybe it was his moccasins which made it possible. Whatever it was, this unearthly power he possessed, one thing was certain. Not one of the great magicians with all of their uncanny feats of levitation, not even the great Blackstone himself, could have accomplished what Yellow Kidney did. But to him it was just all in the day's work.

When the harvest was done, we fed the men. Then Yellow Kidney received his pay and left, without a word, as silent as the hawk in flight. He had been a good hand not to be forgotten. And he was not, for when I returned to the house to help clear the table and wash the dishes, I found his mark—his fingerprints all over the butter!

J. I. Case Thresher—cost $1130.00 in 1925

Threshing late wheat at El Rancho Gumbo, 1929.

STRAWPILE BUCKAROO

CHAPTER 8

Strawpile Buckaroo

WHEN THE OLD stationary threshers were still in use, every wheat rancher had two or three large straw piles. After harvest the livestock got a lot of good feed out of them. These towering piles were also valuable because they afforded protection to the farm animals who could get behind them out of the cold winds. That was very important in this wide open prairie country where there were no trees nor brush anywhere except along the widely spaced rivers. On most of the ranches trees did not show up until well into the thirties when the Federal Government began funding the State Extension Service to furnish shelter belt seedlings to the ranchers.

As the livestock browsed around the piles they eventually trampled the straw down. Then these "straw bottoms", as they were called, became good places to break the new saddle horses. An ornery colt could not buck too hard when he was bogged down in the deep straw and it made a fine landing pad if the rider got dumped. My old cowpunching ancestors from the other century would have called this cheating, but it was a lot more comfortable landing on a pile of straw than on a stony ridge covered with cactus. Besides, it did not pay to take chances or I should say that by 10 a.m. we had already taken more than enough for the day. We were many long and rutted miles from a hospital we could get to at all, and I don't think there was a real ambulance in that part of the state. Pondera County is about 40 miles wide and maybe 100 miles long and at that time had a population of about 4,000 souls, more or less. With neighbors as scarce as warts on a freckled schoolma'am, a rancher alone on a place could have lain for days before being found, and that could have spelled curtains. I remember being marooned for a month in January without seeing anybody.

Any time you are working a green cayuse there are plenty of chances to get busted up. Panic is inherent in most horses, just waiting to be triggered. Whoop-up cowboying might sound exciting to a tenderfoot, but the truth is that in Charlie Russell's time they buried cowboys like they were planting potatoes.

Shortford? 50% Shorthorn plus 50% Hereford
equals 100% Beefsteak. We liked ours grass fed,
three or four years old.

Horses on the Range.

RUNNING WATER

CHAPTER 9

Running Water

IF A RANCHO is to be modern, it should have running water. Running water is an old term used much in the era when houses were just beginning to have plumbing with the water piped in. Before that it was carried in with a bucket.

In a sense, El Rancho Gumbo was modern in its first years. It had running water. But there was a hitch to the situation. The water was not running in quite the same way as the water piped into the modern houses. El Rancho Gumbo's water was, in fact, running down the channel of Two Medicine River, three miles north of the house. It was a plentiful supply, clear, cold and refreshing. And as long as the Great Spirit of the Piegans replenished the snow pack on the ice fields of Glacier National Park and the Sun God melted it down, Two Medicine River kept on running, carrying the pure sweet glacial water down to Maria's River from whence it continued into the Missouri and Mississippi on its way to the Gulf of Mexico.

Because the water was not running into the kitchen, we had to help it get there. The word "kitchen" is a term used with reservation, for it was simply the space where cooking and eating were done in one end of the 12 x 16 foot shack, which we referred to as "the house". Therein, among other handy installations, was a shelf which accommodated the water bucket and wash basin. Beneath the shelf, behind a curtain, one found the "slop bucket", the end of the in-house journey for the water from Two Medicine before it was dumped out the door to the eternal winds of Piegan country.

The chore of hauling water from the river with a team of horses and a wagon took place once a week or so, depending on how quickly we used the water or how we skimped when other jobs were more pressing. There was more than one day at El Rancho Gumbo when we drank sparingly, when water was frugally alloted for dish washing, and everything we ate was fried to negate the need for cooking liquid. During such periods skillets were seldom washed, contending that to do so made the foods stick to them. While this practice was a standard rule of thumb by old time ranch and camp cooks, it stood convenient as an excuse under the circumstances. Our clothes were generally wash-ed in ditch or rain water, but the latter was a rare com-modity.

When the bitter and often treacherous days of winter swirled their snows across the flats, reducing visibility to zero, they brought respite from the lonely treks into the badlands of Two Medicine Valley for water. During those months a barrel was placed beside the old Majestic range in the kitchen, to be packed with snow for the purpose of maintaining a supply of domestic water. The snow was reasonably clean in those pre-toxic pollution days or at least we believed it to be, so there were no purification treatments. We did have days of a different kind of pol-lution which resulted in the snow becoming loaded with solids which would settle to the bottom of a vessel filled with water. This pollution occurred during days and nights when the westerly wind swooped down from the pinnacles of the Rockies and drifted the snow into huge piles filled with soil from the summer-fallowed fields, laying them bare to dry out and become even more vulnerable to the blasts, filling the big sky with a thick pall of dust. This usually happened several days after each big snowfall. Whatever the deal was, any germs ensconced among the particles of gumbo soil must have been blown to Hades and back again because as far as anyone ever knew, none of them ever found haven in our innards.

The trip to the river took about three hours. On nice days during the spring and summer it was not too unpleasant, but in periods of bad weather any journey in an open wagon was nothing but misery. During the summer such expeditions were generally planned to be completed before noon to avoid being in an electrical storm which might bring hail. And it seems there was always a problem. If it wasn't the weather, we were pinched for time or it was something else. On one occasion it was my hat.

At the time I was still a teen-ager and always without money of my own. One of my greatest desires was to acquire a John B. Stetson sombrero, but was unable to do so. I resorted to the next best thing. The small town stores carried limited stocks of most staple goods, but a lot of our purchases were mail orders, and the bulk of our business went to those note-worthy gentlemen referred to as Sears Sawbuck and Monkey Ward, in the lingo of the rural West. We also patronized a midwestern mail order war surplus store. This purveyor of sometimes nondescript World War One merchandise was the recipient of my order for a surplus U.S. Army Cavalry hat and an ischium bruising McClellan army saddle, vintage of General Custer's time, I think. I do not remember exactly what the saddle cost; I think $15, but do recall that the hat was one dollar. It was said to be a new unissued hat and I believe that it was, for it had the appearance of having never been worn or reblocked. I had barely broken it in when my father and I made a trip to the river for water. If it had been an old hat no doubt it would have been jammed onto my noggin, but being quite new yet and stiff, it was not too safely secured. When I leaned over the rear of the wagon to dip up a pail full of water, the hat fell off my head into the swiftly flowing current. Even before I could shout "blankity blank!" it was far downstream, heading for New Orleans. The river was about 300 feet wide at that place, the water was hub deep to our high-wheeled wagon and with the river bed covered with large rocks, precluding speedy pursuit, there wasn't a fiddler's chance of catching up to get it back. It took some time before I could scratch up another dollar for a second order and you had better believe I hung onto that next hat for dear life!

In those days flour came in 50 pound bags made of unbleached muslin. The age of printed patterns on sacks had not yet arrived and the only coloring on them was the name and information alluding to the quality of the product. Flour sacks were valuable items adaptable to many uses as, believe you me, we *really* recycled things in those days. The sacks were always saved to become everything from dish towels to pillow cases and even showed up on clotheslines as ladies' bloomers with the stamp of Four X Quality emblazoned across the rear. The water taken from the river was always strained through a cloth of this material to eliminate the bugs, cottonwood leaves and other foreign matter. But it would be impossible to have a river 100 miles long without some animal life finding it a convenient place to end it all, so there was no way of knowing just how many dead sheep Two Medicine's water was strained through on its way to our barrels. However, there is an old saying that anything out of sight is out of mind, and that axiom was all that we needed. Some "expert", of credentials unknown to us, had already said that the Two Medicine River purified its waters every 50 feet by tumbling over many rocks. This could have been right. At least the tumbling action shook all of the bones out of the water before we dipped it up.

Pieces of canvas, each secured by a hoop, were used to cover the barrels. This kept insects, bird droppings and other assorted miscellany from polluting the water. They also prevented the water from splashing out as the wagon jolted over the rutted roads on our way home.

A well 39 feet deep was drilled in 1925, but as has been said before, it was almost unusable. A sample was sent to the State Health Department for analysis. It was reported to contain high volumes of Epsom Salts, Glauber's salts and common table salts. Epsom salts is bad enough, but Glauber's salts is used by veterinarians and horse breeders as a purgative to relieve chronic constipation in their animals. This water unpleasantly surprised more than one thirsty wayfarer who stopped by to irrigate his parched tonsils on a scorching summer day. Coffee made from it was a slippery muck and washing anything in the slimy liquid was a losing proposition. It rejected soap to the extent that the addition of any kind simply turned to black greasy scum which rose to the surface immediately and clung to our dishrags as if they had been dipped in used crankcase oil. Sandpapering one's beard off would have been preferable to using it for shaving. Oddly enough, the livestock loved the well water and for this reason it was kept pumped enough to keep it usable at all.

SPIKE'S COYOTE

CHAPTER 10

Spike's Coyote

I HAD THIS CRAZY dog named Spike who was some kind of a duke's mixture with an English Shepard. Most sheep dogs have a lot of savvy but for some unknown reason this biscuit biter never did know 'go get em' from a pot of beans. He was scared of his own shadow and usually spent most of his time getting into ridiculous predicaments that he couldn't figure his way out of. On one occasion he ran off to a neighbor's place where some little kids cut off the end of his nose with a butcher knife. That just about put him out of business because a dog has most of his navigation equipment in the end of his nose, and when it is not there anymore he might as well get off the payroll. Another time Spike got scared of a porcupine which everyone knows is the slowest critter in town, and spent the night on top of a hay stack. He could have gone down the other side and been clear out of the county before that rambling pin cushion got wise but he just wouldn't take the chance. Instead, he stayed up there all night and barked at the moon. I had to lift Spike down off the top of the stack the next morning and take him all the way around it to prove to him that the porcupine was nowhere in sight. I'd guess that he must have heard the old story that porcupines throw their quills. We had another dog once who got some quills in his mouth and face trying to bite one of the thorny devils, and our horses sometimes got slapped in the leg so that quills had to be removed, but this was a rare happening.

One day I was heading west on Zam, with Spike coming along behind, to look for some strayed cayuses, when a coyote yapped up by the ridge. Sure enough, Spike figured he needed checking out so he went up to meet him. Well, that coyote came down a ways, and yipping just a little, began to zig and zag and give old Spike the come on. I called Spike to come back but he would not listen. He kept right on letting that blamed coyote make a sucker out of him until they went plum over the top of the ridge which broke off into badlands on the other side. The cut banks were filled with coyote dens and I knew Spike wouldn't have a chance, so I swung Zam up to the top and began yelling my brains out. No dog or coyote was in sight by the time we got there. After a half hour of yelling I was getting pretty hoarse and it looked like "goodbye Spike", so I turned Zam around and we went sadly on our way. I felt pretty bad about it because I could see that coyote having Spike's short ribs for lunch. He wasn't worth much but I wouldn't have wished all of that onto him for anything.

We had not gone far when suddenly there was the goldangest yipping and ki-yi-ing anybody ever heard. Zam snorted and picked up his ears as we both looked up towards the ridge. There was Spike coming down the hill with his tail between his legs and both ears flapping in the breeze. And just inches behind him was that coyote, snapping at his heels. They were coming so fast that we didn't have time to get out of the way and that crazy Spike ran right through under Zam's belly. And I swear, if I hadn't waved my hand and yelled, that danged coyote would have gone right on through also. He must have been concentrating so much on the dog that he didn't even see Zam and me, but when I bellowed he just set all four brakes and slid on his seat like old Casey coming into third base at the World Series. If he had been wearing pants he would have ripped the seat right out of them. Of course when all of this happened so suddenly, the way it did, Zambeezie panicked and being a spooky cuss anyway, shied off to one side, almost dumping me right in old Mr. Coyote's lap.

It took a little time to get organized again. While I was busy getting Zam back to earth, the coyote, figuring he had gotten in too deep, swung about and got out of there plum pronto. By the time I got most of my anatomy back on top of Zam, Spike had pooped out and there he was, lying flat in the buffalo grass, his tongue out a foot and he was panting like a steam engine. For the rest of that trip he made it a point to stay mighty close to Zam and me because that ruckus turned out to be the biggest lesson he ever learned. And from that day on, whenever Spike heard a coyote howl, he was right up on top of that hay stack again, barking back—braver than a Brahma bull!

OUTLAW FIGHTS BACK

CHAPTER 11

Outlaw Fights Back

LIKE A LOT OF them who grew up in the wide open spaces, Old Killer was plum salty and half-handy. He probably weighed more than 1500 pounds, which was a hefty hunk of horse to wrestle any day. When you got your rope on one of those big guys a real battle could bust loose. It was not like fiddling around with an awkward hand-raised colt who was feeling his oats. These horses were rebellious because they were wild. It was the same as if you had caught a grizzly bear or a bull elk. Killer was not young and the chances are that he had felt a rope only once or twice in his whole life when he was branded or cut. And he had probably completely demolished every corral he was shagged into, if he was corralled at all. If he was a stud horse, he was twice as nasty, a great big bundle of dynamite, exploding all over the place. In spite of his ferocity, he was a handsome horse which made it all the harder to leave him alone. And his vicious nature, instilled by a life of freedom, made him determined to resist all attempts to subdue him.

Fresh off the range, Killer was a real diamond in the rough. He was born on the range, lived his life on the range and may die on the range without ever having been groomed in any way. The outlaw's mane and tail were knotted and tangled and sometimes dragged the ground. His hooves were outgrown and gumbo dried with split and jagged edges. His fetlocks, loaded with hard dried balls, rattled like castanets. Wandering over the gumbo flats he had picked up gobs of it, and golf balls of mud dried in his tail sometimes inflicted a painful injury when a swatch of hair flipped around a hock to hang in a half hitch, cutting the flesh to the bone.

The long, snarled mane often presented a problem when the horse was roped. It was necessary to be sure that the honda eye of the lariat was not too small because if it was, and a bunch of tangled mane hair was pulled through, it could knot up tight. If that happened, the bronc would have to be choked until he dropped so the rope could be cut to get it off. During the whole ruckus, feet were flying everywhere, and you had better watch those front ones. They were lightning fast and could spell sudden death in capital letters. It was never a one-man job, but took two or three to get him down, because while one man was snubbing him to the post, another would try to front foot Old Killer and somehow flip the rope over his shoulder and trip him with a quick jerk. Once down, an ear was grabbed and his nose pinched as the head was pulled over and back. This usually put him out of commission for a shortwhile, but he had to be let up soon because it is murder to keep a horse down too long. It was a rambunctious battle all the way and sometimes a guy was lucky if he had any corral left after the fracas was over.

One of the most interesting parts of life on a ranch is the contingent of interesting and comical characters. El Rancho Gumbo had its share. High on the roster was Tarzan, our old blue cat, who couldn't miss anything. No matter how wild and woolly the party got, Tarzan was always there. And one thing was for sure, we never could have gotten the job done without his supervision and advice.

The Last Coyote Hunt

This black mare was Tubby's daughter, and was foaled at El Rancho Gumbo on the same day that Helen Jane True (Mrs. Harold Johnson) was born at Kalispell, Montana. Her name was Nig, one that we would not consider using now that we have learned to respect the ethnic origins of others.

BORN IN A BLIZZARD

CHAPTER 12

Born in a Blizzard

UPS AND DOWNS are a way of life in the ranching business. During one of the downs at El Rancho Gumbo the cattle herd vanished, to the last cow. Later, after some changes in the family structure, I was on my own way up.

The old-time art of horse trading was giving way to car swapping and I was doing my part in developing the new science. I had never owned a new automobile but had my share of the oldies. After going through an Overland, two Whippets and an Essex, I acquired a fourth or fifth hand 1926 Model 58 Chrysler coach (two door sedan). It was a huge contraption with a four-cylinder Maxwell engine and two-wheel brakes. Predating the fuel pump, this car was dependent upon a vacuum tank to supply the carburetor. As a safety feature, a gadget in the crankcase was connected to the vacuum system to interrupt the gasoline flow if the oil level dropped, to prevent damage to the engine. However, my car was beyond further damage. It steered badly, the brakes were shot, the doors would not stay latched, and the engine was so worn that it gulped oil by the bucketful. To keep the fuel flowing, I carried a five gallon can of used eighty-weight tractor oil, which I administered several times on each trip to town and back. Finally, in desperation, the ghost took off, leaving my Chrysler dead in its tracks half-way between the house and the barn.

Dan Culletin, who lived west of Valier, owned a Chrysler which was the same model as mine. He needed parts, but like everyone else was short on wampum, so one blizzardy day, by the warmth of the pot bellied stove in Tom Haugen's pool hall, a deal was struck. Dan got my Chrysler and I was back in the cattle business with a skinny black and white mulie heifer, said to be partly of Polled Shorthorn ancestry. She was barely two-years old and already pregnant. Penelope, as I named her, was so thin she could be seen from a side view only. Finding herself to be the only cow and me the only person-animal on El Rancho Gumbo, she immediately formed a close attachment, and I to her. I couldn't give her diamonds or roses so I stuffed her with hay from an ample supply I was lucky to have on hand. Penelope began to swell and to show her appreciation for my kindness to her, followed me about, licking the seat of my Levi's whenever I stopped.

So indelibly recorded in my memory was the advent of Penelope's first born that I dared not fail to include it in this work. It was one of those January days with the mercury hanging out the bottom of the thermometer and a whingdinger of a blizzard was just tapering off. About noon I had examined Penelope for the six-hour warning but had missed the signal. Leaving her in care of Tubby, the old reliable chore pony, many times a mother, I left the stable and went back to the house. At four o'clock I returned to the stable. The corral gate had blown open and there was no Penelope. Braving the blowing snow, I made a fast check of the barnyard but did not find her. Recalling that she had been doing some investigating up west lately, I threw the saddle on Tubby and taking an extra blanket, headed that way. We found Penelope, a mile from home, in a bunch of willows by the ditch bank, with this little bugger still wet and shivering himself plum loco. When we arrived, his ma started running around in circles, with the placenta still dragging, bawling and making a great big fuss. I bundled the calf up and almost busted a gut hoisting him onto the saddle even though I had parked Tubby in a shallow field ditch to lower her about a foot. Then I climbed on board behind him. I still can't figure how I got both of us up there, the calf in a blanket and me with my big sheepskin coat and four buckle Arctics, but I did and we headed for home. By this time it was getting dark and Tubby stumbled when she lost her horizon in the blank-out. At the stable I stood the little guy up to suck but he just collapsed, flat as a pancake. I thought for sure that he was a goner and all I could say was "Aw, hell!" I wiped him dry and covered him to get warm. Penelope got mad at me for putting the blanket over him because she wanted to lick him, but she soon simmered down and got interested in some hay. She had lost the after-birth somewhere in the dark on the way in, so now she was in pretty good shape and already starting to get over it. I named the little guy Ol' Bliz because he had been born in a blizzard and surprising it was, for having such a skinny mama, he grew into the biggest red steer on Fisher Flats.

When the spring thaw came, Penelope made love again and in December of that same year presented me with another red bouncing baby bull. I now had three head of cattle, you might say in one year. I wanted heifers but steers meant cash, so I was happy enough. That old Chrysler, with all of its faults, turned out to be the luckiest car I ever owned!

PIEGAN HORSE

CHAPTER 13

Piegan Horse

THE BENCH P PONY was typical of many of the range
horses. Not all of them were the big chunks. They came in
all shapes and sizes and a wide variety of colors. There were
Calico Pintos, Mouse, Buckskin, Appaloosa and Duns or
whatever.

The Piegan Tribal brand, shown on the hip, was known
as the Bench P: the letter P standing on a bench. The bench
probably came from the bench topography of the area.
Benches are long, low, flat topped ridges or table lands
formed by glacial and wind action. The letter "P" stood for
Piegan. I do not recall which hip it was on. Verbal investi-
gation sheds no light.

The Bench P pony was immortalized in song at the time
of the big round-up when all of the horses on the Blackfeet
reservation were dipped for range itch. Many were sold to
cannery buyers. A lyric was written by the deputy sheriff
at Browning, to be sung to the tune of *Cheyenne*.

We owned a long rangy, hardkeeping Bench P pony.
He was a bay color and his frame indicated a slight possibil-
ity of distant Hambletonian ancestors. Tom, as we called
him, after Tom Little Wolf who sold him to us, was an extremely ill-mannered horse, unreliable and untrustworthy.
We were told, at the time of purchase, that he could be

ridden or used as a work animal. This was true to a degree only, and it proved to be Tom's undoing. One day while cultivating the potato patch, he ran away with the cultivator, reducing it to a pile of mangled junk and tearing himself up so badly that my brother got down his 250-3000 Savage rifle and eliminated Tom on the spot.

My brother with one of the
mares in 1927

SOD BUSTER AT WORK

Plowing up El Rancho Gumbo with the 1928 Model K, 18-32 horsepower J.I. Case tractor. Its powerful four-cylinder engine was mounted crosswise just like the modern automobiles of today. Few tractors were ever built with the quality this one had.

Too Many Uncles

CHAPTER 14

Too Many Uncles

TARZAN, THE CAT and my dog, Spike, were not the only anomalous characters occupying stations of importance at El Rancho Gumbo. During the years that spanned my tour of duty there, we bought, raised, sold and lost something like 200 head of horses, more or less. Some were not around long enough to develop any great amount of notable character. Others, such as the original cadre, if I may call them that, were what one might refer to as "built in fixtures". Being genuine integral parts of El Rancho Gumbo, they could not help absorbing its influence by taking on a wide variety of idiosyncracies which would be unbelievable to people not accustomed to living with animals.

Dick and Major were the two most reliable old standbys. As steady as two Rocks of Gibraltar, they would willingly give their all in times of need. If anything several times their weights was movable at all, they would move it. Docile to an extreme degree, they would harm nothing, never ever kicking, biting, striking, stomping or running away, no matter how hairy the situation became. Even a baby was safe in their presence.

Major was a Clydesdale stag, having headed up another rancher's stud as a young horse, who had been altered prior to coming to El Rancho Gumbo. He was the larger of the team, typically Clyde, dark brown color with long flat boned legs having plenty of white feather. His stride was long and he always kept his traces tight. Never, at any time did he ever do one thing to arouse one's ire, and was sorely missed when he died at the age of 20, just a couple of years before I left. His death was due to uremic poisoning caused by eating frozen wheat.

If Major was the "horseification" of a perfect gentleman, Dick was anything but that. Notwithstanding the wee bit of integrity which prompted him to co-operate with his team mate in pulling out a stuck load, Dick was so lazy there was no limit to the ideas he would come up with to avoid a little bit of labor. He not only was lazy, he even looked lazy. He was a heavy boned Shire of dubious ancestry. Bay in color, his piano legs were covered to his hocks, in true Shire fashion, with an even heavier growth of coarse black hair than his partner's. His head was huge and generally hung at an elevation as to make him appear absolutely flat on top; that is, if a two by four had been layed from between his ears to his rump it would have been exactly level. His neck was straight, minus the crest arch of well endowed draft animals, which added to his ungainly profile. Dick was no beauty, but he was all horse, if lazy.

For some reason he hated field work with a vengeance. And his worst behavior was always manifest when he was assigned to a position in a multiple hitch, generally anything from a four to eight horse hook-up. Due to this adversity, Dick was never driven in the lead, but his wheel position was not the answer either because it allowed him to lag. He would stroll along as leisurely as possible, deviously dreaming up one ridiculous idea after another to keep from straining himself. His favorite schemes included such habits as biting at an imaginary fly on his foreleg, even in chilling weather when no flies were out, bumping the lead team eveners or having a prolonged series of carefully orchestrated answers to nature's call which required considerably reduced speed. However bad his conduct in the field, his redeeming grace lay in his stoic manner which made him the best danged anchor horse in the whole county. Today T.V. newscasters are proud of their anchor positions, but let no one be misinformed, they are not new because Dick had pioneered the art many years before the birth of today's profession. Whenever a new and often miserably ornery horse was broken to work he was "bucked back to" (tied or chained from his bridle to Dick's near hame), rendering the wild one incapable of getting out of hand. It was like being anchored to a cubic yard of solid concrete. There was no way a runaway could happen.

Most of the livestock at El Rancho Gumbo were gloriously healthy, seldom knowing a day of sickness, Major's untimely passing being a rare exception. Pampering was not practiced and the mares and cows usually gave birth to their young out there under the big sky. If a cow was lucky enough to calve when all of the old-timers were at work, everything was hunky-dory. But if a cow's timing coincided with their day off, that was a different story and she didn't have a chance. The old boys were right there, en masse, Tom, Dick and Buster and all of the others too. Crowding around the newly arrived, who was barely able to stand on his wobbly little legs, they gently nuzzled the calf as they checked him out, preventing the mother from getting anywhere near him. It was just like those old geldings figured that the cow didn't know the first dad-burned thing about starting a calf out in life, and they were going to make sure that he got off on the right foot or they would know the reason why! And everything did come out just fine because no serious circumstances ever resulted from these scenarios; it was a regular occurrence, all in the day's work.

During the final days of horse farming, I procured a set of plans for a six-horse hitch, from the Horse Association of America. It was set up for two three-horse teams in such a way that it was virtually impossible for any horse in the team to goof off. Dick's heart was broken and the sadness of his sighs almost disabled me with remorse—but not quite.

The author with one of
the last "windbellies"

MILKING TIME

CHAPTER 15

Milking Time

WHEN THE CATTLE business got going again, I'd guess it could be said that El Rancho Gumbo was diversified. It produced both milk and beef, but the six-cow dairy herd could not be compared to the one at Carnation Farm. Every kind except Water Buffalo, the cows ran out on the open range and had minds of their own. Two big reds from the Sweetgrass Hills were spooky as all get out. One, especially, was a female snake, and my first attempt to milk her ended with me below and cow on top. It took a lot of molar grinding and perseverance plus some pretty strong palaver, but in the end I conquered her.

The dairy barn was a shed roofed building with a platform floor and homemade two-by-four stanchions for six cows. There was also a calf pen at one end of the building. Because El Rancho Gumbo was now a one-man operation, all work was planned to be as streamlined as possible. To avoid shoveling barn flakes in good weather, all milking was done outside in the corral, where there were no stanchions. This often required the use of other methods to hold old Bossie long enough to extract the juice. By lashing both ends to the posts and pinning her tightly to the corral with my head in her flank, I was able to induce her to give down the milk after no more than a half-dozen stanzas of

[75]

the *Red River Valley*. Kicking, bucket jumping and butting were not the only occupational hazards encountered by the milker. Others included a slap in the face with a loaded tail brush or being urinated on by a thoughtless heifer passing by behind.

One thing had to be said for these cows, they were healthy, never knowing a day of illness, and the raw milk was consumed at home without any thought of problems. Everything must have been O.K., because I am writing this 50-years later and am not sick yet. However, the dairy angle was only a passing part of the cow business; the real intent was to build up a herd of big reds for beef and this project was well on its way when I called it quits.

After taking out some milk for myself and Tarzan, the balance of it was separated and the skimmed milk went to the pigs, chickens, or calves. Once a week I hauled a five gallon can full of 36% butterfat cream to the Valier creamery and sold it for $1.75. Not much, I admit, but it was the only cash flow until harvest time. All through the depression we lived on paper at the store, garage, fuel depot and machinery house. Only in the fall when wheat, a steer or two, and maybe some useless range horses were sold, was the paper taken care of. At the bottom of the depression our wheat, which was graded Number One Dark Hard Northern Spring—the nation's highest—got down to $.16 a bushel on track at the local elevators. There were months on end when one had no cash at all, which is why the little cream check was appreciated.

Zambeezie as a four-year-old, in his winter coat. He was Tubby's son, sired by Comet. Shown here in 1931 with the author.

My visiting Aunt Lucy Meitner with Kit, a 1900-pound black Percheron mare. This mare, with her black gelding team mate, was later sold and shipped to Montreal, Canada.

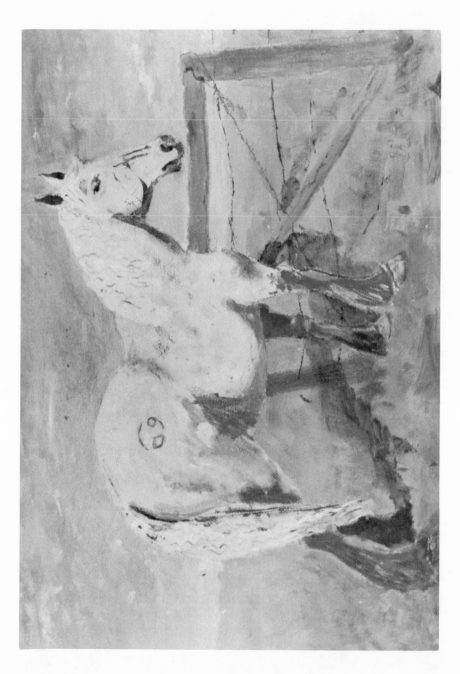

COMET

CHAPTER 16

Percheron Pappy

THE LARGE POPULATION of horses on the Blackfeet reservation could not all be blamed on the government or the Piegans. Neighbors, both good and bad, have been at the bottom of more than one funny deal in this world. There was a distinct shortage of policemen and deputy sheriffs and a lot of open country with no one in sight. Under these circumstances it was not hard for ranchers who lived off the reservation and had more horses than they needed at home, to shove them across the rivers to enjoy the free Buffalo grass, courtesy of the Piegans. Sometimes the horses were driven over without the owner's knowledge, but whatever the reason, they were there and the reservation became their home.

My Percheron stallion, Comet, was a Quarter Circle Diamond Nine horse from Seven Mile Coulee. Along with two others, a half-brother and a half-sister, he had disappeared from Pat Mills' pasture when they were long yearlings and had not been seen since. When the big dappled gray gelding tangled in our fence and sustained a severe wire cut wound, we brought him in to doctor the leg. I don't remember when the word got to Pat but he and his two boys had been looking out our way and showed up in a couple of days. They were overjoyed to find the horses as

[79]

Pat had been trying to find them so they could be sold. I took a fancy to the horses and prevailed upon my Dad to put up the cash, and we bought them on the spot.

These horses were all the same age, that is five years old. Comet was a light dappled gray with gun metal legs and weighed just under 1600 pounds in lean range shape. The gelding, Prince, was a darker dappled gray and somewhat heavier than Comet, being a thicker horse and deeper in the chest and body. Pansy, the mare, was the least showy of the three. She was a darker blue and was inclined to carry her head lower so that she had a flatter top line plus a wide flat rump splattered with buttermilk. She was the hardest keeper of the bunch. All had good legs with flat bones.

Comet had a rope on only once when he was branded as a yearling, and was one tough nut to break. It took a 20-foot mule skinner (shot loaded blacksnake whip) to straighten him out. He was a one-man horse and I was the only one who could put a harness on him. Some are like that. If any other did try to harness him they risked a kick in the teeth. Even I could not walk up to Comet in the corral and slip a halter or rope onto him. The only way he could be had was with a loud pop of the snapper on the end of the blacksnake. That would make him head for his stall in the stable. As soon as he was there, the problem ended.

During the time that I had Comet, he sired several fine colts. They were all thrifty and spirited animals, easy to handle except one. The odd one was Zambeezie, whose mother was Tubby, the old chore pony. She had already had a dozen before him. His behavior was no fault of hers but due strictly to his birth defect.

About this time talking movies had not been around too long and whenever a few pennies could be scratched together, we headed for the movie in town. It was not hard to become a fan since the girls on the screen were pretty and the male actors extremely macho. The influence had to be reflected somewhere and on El Rancho Gumbo that place was in the barnyard. All of the colts ended up with names of stars. The corral roster included Jean Harlow, Clark Gable, Betty Grable, Eleanor Powell and Gary Cooper, among others.

The time arrived when horses, especially draft types, were no longer in demand. When the horse business declined, I stagged Comet and sold him to a buyer who shipped him to Harrisburg, Pennsylvania. I'll bet that at least *one* Amishman learned to swear!

THE BIG DIP

CHAPTER 17

The Big Dip

WHEN THE HUGE one-and-two cylinder kerosene and steam tractors were banging away turning the first sod of the prairies, horses were used for all of the work that followed, such as harrowing, seeding, cutting and hauling of the grain crops. After the big engines had broken the prairie, a period of "stubbling in" lasted for several years. This term came from the practice of merely pulling a horse-drawn disc harrow over the stubble, then planting the next crop without replowing the fields. Eventually the land had to be plowed again and the farmers began riding into the depression on smaller three and four plow tractors. They had steel wheels with lugs and most of them had four cylinder engines, although John Deere continued to manufacture small two-cylinder tractors which were exceedingly efficient. These distillate burning tractors rapidly replaced teams of four to ten horses. A few odd job horses were around for awhile, but being used less and less, finally left the scene entirely. A tractor was a lot easier to handle than a bunch of horses, and did more work because it could travel at a steadier pace and there was no limit on hours. It never tired and all it needed was a little more go juice plus a shot of grease, and with a change of operators it could work around the clock. Besides these advantages, the driver was higher up and in front of the machinery where there was less dust than when he rode low, behind the team.

The horse and mule population reached its peak in the State of Montana in 1926 when it was reported to be 576,000 horses and 11,000 mules. Since then it declined to a mere fraction of that, but there were still a lot of horses on the Blackfeet reservation by 1930. It was about that time when range itch, also known as scabies, was found among the animals, and the federal authorities ordered that all horses on the reservation must be dipped at government expense. My brother and I, along with two of our neighbors, took all of our horses and those of several other neighbors up to the dip. The vat was about 20-miles west of El Rancho Gumbo, on Badger Creek, west of the Yellowstone-Glacier Beeline highway. The bunch numbered about 50 head and we stayed overnight at the Old Agency Irrigation camp.

For some reason this event was allowed to pass undocumented by both local officials and residents. Repeated attempts to recover dates and other information about the dip have failed, although I feel sure there has to be some historical date or local data somewhere.

After a considerable amount of research I finally obtained a copy of a letter from the Commissioner of Indian Affairs in Washington D.C. to Hon. John R. Mohler, Chief of the Bureau of Animal Husbandry, thanking him for his report that 4,914 horses had been dipped and that the job was now completed. The letter mentions date June 17 but does not give the year. Some generous stamping by a file clerk shows it was filed on June 24 (and) 25, 1932, but either obliterates the date of the commissioner's letter, or it was not indicated. At any rate, this date does not fit into my recollections because of my memory of people present at the round-up. Other items such as car models and an injury sustained by one of our mares seem to be in conflict and predate this filing. I was there and remember all kinds of word of mouth estimates, exceeding the number of animals recorded. However, I would not dare to guess, but do know there were an awful lot of horses there, all the way up Badger Creek, as far as I could see.

GREEN GRASS ROMEO

CHAPTER 18

Green Grass Romeo

ZAMBEEZIE HAD A nasty habit of rearing when I hit
the saddle. He figured that if he dumped me he could take
the day off, but it didn't work that way. I got wise to him
early and always left enough of the knotted end of my
hard twist lariat hang loose for use as a whammer to deck
him so he wouldn't go over backwards on me. A rearing
horse is too dangerous to play around with. For as long as
I had Zam we never began any day without first going
through that ritual. I never owned a martingale and rigged
some jerry-mandered deals, but they were more trouble
than they were worth.

One day we met my neighbor Jim driving his funny
pair of mousey little mares on an empty wagon. Jim was a
jolly fellow, always laughing and never without his old
Wellington pipe, the kind which looked like a saxaphone.
The mares, no doubt, had been little queens in better days
but now, pot-bellied and swayed, they were past their prime
and hardly what could be called candidates for romance.
But that danged Zam didn't care what others thought, and
right away began to get smart alecky and all. I reined him
in but his stomping and snorting around excited the mares
and when they began to fidget, Jim set the brake. We pow-
wowed for several minutes, discussing the spring seeding

and a few other things until the horses all got so restless that we decided to end our visit.

When we got ready to go on our ways, I started to swing Zam around, but he just jerked the bit and jumped right up into the wagon with his front feet, upsetting the seat and knocking Jim end over stew kettle into the back of the box. Jim's hat and pipe went sailing. The first thing that hit my mind was a signal to unload pronto because I knew I could never stay aboard and get him out of there without both of us getting busted up. I managed to hang onto him and step into the wagon while Jim was picking himself up. Luckily, Jim wasn't hurt, but that red-hot string of expletives which emanated from my neighbor were all brand new ones which had never been heard before. He really expressed his opinion of my horse in no uncertain terms, and I can't say that I could blame him for doing so. The mares bolted but with the brake set they could not get far. However, they continued to put on a first class Hula-Hula performance until Jim could get hold of the lines again and quiet them down. Somehow, by hook or crook, we managed to get my knothead out of the wagon. I don't know yet how we did it without him getting hung up in a wheel and breaking a leg. I'd guess he was just too ornery to break anything.

I forget to say it was spring and the green grass was just too much for the goofey Romeo. I sold him later to Gene Leach who shipped him to Snohomish, Washington, where the grass is always green. I hope that Zam lived happily ever after!

ALBERT WARNER OPERATING a Ruth Dredger, cleaning silt from an irrigation canal. These machines were built by the Ruth Dredger Manufacturing Company of Huntington Park, California, and the Blackfeet Project purchased one of the first ones made. Walter True was the first operator. Others, besides Warner, included my brother Marion, Ray Scott and Ole Olson who was transferred, with my father, to construction of the Tongue River Project on the Northern Cheyenne Reservation in 1933. The machine shown here was operated by the Valier Land and Water Company, a Carey Act project, across Birch Creek, south of the Blackfeet reservation. Marion later worked for the Ruth Dredger factory when he first left Montana.

[89]

STANDOFF

CHAPTER 19

Standoff

ON EL RANCHO GUMBO every operation was a serious project. It was like a factory with different departments. Each one had to produce a certain part. An attempt was made to produce the biggest part of that which was consumed at home. Vegetables were raised and stored, meat was cured, and eggs layed in the spring and summer were preserved for winter in an aqueous plastic called "water glass". A trip to the store one or more times a day was out. Most of the time once a week was more like it. Sometimes the winter lay-in of non-home grown supplies was ordered by mail and hauled from town by the wagon load. The poultry department was closely guarded against marauding coyotes and hawks, and every hen having the slightest inclination to lay an egg was treated with the utmost respect.

Hardly a day went by without some kind of a rambunctious happening. The meddlesome calf had just raided the hen house and chased the hens off their nests. That wasn't too good for the egg laying business. The chore pony had wandered off and I was on foot, when I discovered the robbery in progress. I undertook to get El Torrito out of the hen house and into the corral. I should have gotten my rope and dabbed a loop on him, but didn't, and just tried to haze him over to where the corral gate was, but the calf had other ideas. I chased him this way and that until I was pooped, and finally picked up a feed bucket that was sitting by the corral, and bounced it off his head. Turning around and spreading his feet, he just stood there and dared me to go further. Sometimes a guy got so mad that he just wanted to sit down on the bucket and cry, but you generally let off the head of steam with a string of oaths made up of letters you can't find in our alphabet. It was a good thing that the nearest preacher was 18 miles away because he sure would have heard it all if he had been any closer.

Anyway, the latch on the hen house door was fixed so the raider could not get in again; but then something else happened the next day. I can't recall now what it was. There was never a dull moment.

The ditchrider's daughter, Helen Jane
True. She invited Dad and me to come
to their house for angel *foot* cake.

CHAPTER 20

Sheepwagon

SHEEPWAGONS WERE A common sight on Montana's prairies. These covered wagons were Home Sweet Home to more than one sheepherder. They were not the type used by the pioneers in their westward push, but were more the grand-daddies of our modern travel trailers. Carried on conventional farm wagon gear, the sheepwagon was blanketed under the canvas cover and fitted with a tin stove, cupboard, and table which drew out from under the bed across the rear. The campjack (tender) moved the wagon periodically as the sheep band moved over the range. Other people also used sheep wagons for temporary abodes. I have lived in one, with another boy, while repairing fence for the old Park Saddle Horse Company. The Long and Clary Sheep Company's lease on the reservation abutting three sides of El Rancho Gumbo was said to cover a lot of acres from there westward toward the mountains for a distance of 28 miles. The next nearest abode in that direction was the sub-Indian agency, known as the "Old Agency", which was beyond Kip's Coulee and at a distance of 14 miles.

Prior to the manufacture of man made fibers sheep ranching was a profitable business, being a two-crop venture of both lambs and wool. However, sheep were not without problems, the biggest one being the constant threat of range depletion. This was said to have sparked the range wars of earlier years. Cows and horses do no harm if properly managed but sheep are a lot different. They run from spot to spot until well into the day, each one trying to beat the other to the next blade of grass, before settling down to serious grazing. Their hooves are sharp and they take many steps, actually cutting the grass out at the roots. An average band, at that time, was 2,000 to 3,000 head and a double band was 4,000 or more, so you can readily see possibilities of some range depletion even in a single pass over. The range was fragile and had to be carefully managed, so the sheep were moved across it systematically. I recall Paddy Flaherty, a local sheepherder (and coal mine cook), telling me that the L & C Company ran a total of 60,000 head of sheep. I don't know if this is a correct figure or not. I have been away for a long time and our old friend Paddy has been in heaven for many years.

After leaving El Rancho Gumbo, I bounced around a lot and one of my first jobs, in 1936, was fence builder and truck driver for the Bar X 6, The Park Saddle Horse Company. I remember my partner well but his name escapes me. I do know that he was a son-in-law of Adolf Norman who lived on Milk River, north of Browning. We got along well and repaired a lot of fence that spring. We were camped out by Duck Lake and our work team was a pair of older pack horses who would work also. After work they were hobbled, and turned loose for the night, so we could catch them the next day as the Duck Lake range covered many acres.

Our work wagon was a light one which we trailed behind the sheepwagon whenever we moved camp, but one day we left it out on the fence line and rode the horses in, figuring to move the next morning. I don't know what happened that morning because while I was washing up the breakfast dishes, my partner caught up the horses, harnessed them and hitched them to our abode, wrong side to; that is, he inadvertently put the right hand horse on the left side and vice versa. I didn't notice this and when we started out to move, those ponies didn't like the mix-up and they took off hell bent for election. There were a lot of big rocks covering the land and they sure didn't try to miss any of them. The way we bounced over them and flew through the air between the boulders was something to remember. The horses were going so hard that my buddy could not handle them so I grabbed one line and he took the other and it took both of us sawing on those ribbons to get them stopped. Well, during the run-a-way we bounced so hard that all of the tin dishes and pots and pans flew out of the cupboard, along with most of the grubstake. For the rest of that job we had tapioca pancakes for breakfast every morning because we just scooped everything up and dumped it all in sacks together. That was all we could do.

Until the middle thirties, grass range on the Blackfeet Reservation leased for ten cents an acre. Stockmen figured 22-acres per cow and a ratio of six sheep to one cow. Farm land leased for $1.50 an acre for land under the ditch, and $1.00 for land above the ditch. Then out-bidding started, and you know the rest of the story. Things have been going up ever since. I wouldn't know how to go back and get started again. Strange as it now seems, in the early years things were tough, yet it was not too hard to get going if you had a wagon and four horses. I remember one neighbor telling how he came down from the High Line (along the Great Northern Railway, east of Shelby) with his team and nothing but a shirt. He said he didn't need any pants because he was standing in a grain tank and the ladies couldn't see his bare parts. I think that will do for this time.

Chief Whiteman, circa 1910

CHAPTER 21

Chief Whiteman

CHIEF WHITEMAN WAS typical of the old-time members of the Piegan tribe. They were men of high moral character who lived by a strict code of ethics. Beside Whiteman, I had the pleasure of knowing Eli Gardepi, Heavy Breast, Ironeater, Running Crane, Two Guns Whitecalf and others. I also remember Grandma Eagle Calf, Wades In Water, and Chases After Buffalo. I still have, hanging on the wall, a beaded buckskin pouch made by Grandma Coldfeet about 1910. I recall our father taking us to a Round Dance, held somewhere east of Browning when I was three or four years old, and sitting on the knee of one of the old chiefs. I do not remember who he was, but he could very well have been Whiteman.

The Piegans accepted my father, not only as their Dirt Boss on the construction of the Blackfeet Irrigation Project, but as their friend and family counselor as well. Being human, just like the Paleface, they were not immune to family arguments and often sought him as a mediator. Eventually, he was initiated into the Crazy Dog chapter of the tribe as an honorary member and was called Chief Ironhand because his right hand was missing and he wore an iron hook with a boot-top sleeve, fashioned by the camp blacksmith. Dad's Indian name was Mukskimyucksi. This is as near as I can spell it.

J. G. WAGNER
(CHIEF IRONHAND)
1911

Standing, left to right: J.M. Long, Commissary clerk; Chas. Dillon, Canal foreman; O.A. Huff, sub-foreman; J.O. Lathou, sub-foreman; R.J. Oliver, Blacksmith; Ed Schadt, sub-foreman; F.O. Russel, Ass't Blacksmith; J.C. Gilman, sub-foreman; I.G. Wagner, General Foreman; Fred Higtimekeeper. Seated, left to right: — Thornburg, sub-foreman; B. Osborn, Canal rider; — Philips, sub-foreman; * — Mickle, sub-foreman; — Kennedy, sub-foreman; * — Burnesson, Carpenter foreman; * C.W. Honald, Assistant carpenter

CHIEF IRONHAND AND HIS GANG

These men were over-seers of a crew of Blackfeet (Piegan) Indian men working about 500 horses and government mules on plows, slip scrapers, fresnos and graders, excavating several hundred miles of canals which became the Blackfeet Irrigation Project. R.C. (Ralph) Bricker later was secretary of the Great Falls Chamber of Commerce and also served in the Montana State Legislature. He put mouse traps in Dad's pockets for a joke.

My father had written these names on the back of the original photo which was in bad shape. Some of the names are doubtful. Those marked with an asterisk (*) may not be correct.

Prior to his government service, Dad was a railway passenger conductor on the Chicago, Burlington and Quincy Railroad. When I was two months old, he was injured in a railway mishap, near Crow Agency, Montana, which resulted in the amputation of his right hand. For being disabled, he was discharged from their service. Two years later he went to work as General Field Foreman on the construction of the Blackfeet Irrigation project. This eventually led to the beginning of El Rancho Gumbo. He retired from federal service at age 65. He passed away in 1956 during his 81st year.

Mother was a farmer and had a nice bunch of cattle started, about thirty head, including two purebred Hereford cows. When she died, Dad was panic stricken and sold the entire herd to pay the medical bills and the undertaker's note. They had no medical insurance in those days and no life insurance policy for mother. Vic Starr, the funeral director, admonished Dad for dispersing the herd, stating that he was not one bit worried about non-payment of the note. But Dad had never owed a bill and, due to his disability, always feared unemployment. He could not cope with a debt. He was widely known among construction men of his time as the most efficient, cost-cuttingest irrigation man to be found anywhere, completing many jobs ahead of schedule and under budget estimate. His workers praised him for his fairness and friendliness as a boss.

BIG MACK

CHAPTER 22

Big Mack

HORSES ARE LIKE people, some are intelligent, kindly and willing to work and pay for their keep. Others are pig-headed, ornery and dedicated to making life miserable for themselves and everybody around them. We had every kind and as I said before, we raised more horses by accident than most people did on purpose.

Mack had all of the disqualifications listed above and a few more besides. First of all he *was* an accident. He was long and tall with a glass eye and a Roman nose. His ugly hide, halfway between a sorrel and a buckskin, was draped over a rack of bones that all of the oats and hay in the State of Montana couldn't put an ounce of fat on. Son of Daisy, an old halter-puller, and an itinerant cayuse pappy, he had inherited all of the bad habits of both. Mack refused to be led or to work with other horses. He was so stubborn that he could literally freeze in any position, and Satan himself could not have budged him. I should have sold him as a statue to stand in the town square with General Grant in the saddle.

After what I had been through so far on El Rancho Gumbo I wasn't going to let Mack get the best of me. There had to be a way to bring him around—and there was. I had read in the *Farm Life* Magazine that horses pulling the

Dynamometer at the Illinois State Fair had developed an average of ten drawbar horsepower, each. I had it! Our Case tractor was rated at 18 horsepower on the drawbar. This was my answer. I harnessed up Big Mack and fitted him with my loveliest peg tooth harrow. Then, after giving him a swift, friendly kick in the rear, chained him to the plow behind the tractor and took off across the west forty. He soon found it useless to argue with J.I. Case and I never looked back. When I finished plowing the field, he had it nicely harrowed and even condescended to be led to water.

Several months later, I sold Big Mack to a buyer who shipped him to Honolulu. The big dumbbell was all gut and always hungry. I sincerely hope that he didn't eat the grass skirts off the girls at Waikiki!

Dad with "Lillums" and foal, 1926

We called my brother "M.F." He's pictured here with Daisy and an "Onion", a term for "young one" used by Indian friend Oliver Racine.

Forty Below

CHAPTER 23

Forty Below

WHEN WINTER CAME to Piegan country it often hit
with a vengeance. October's first half had been a beautiful
autumn with the bluest skies in the whole world. Of all the
places I have ever been, no other surpassed the Big Sky of
Montana. It was 1934 and my father had come up from the
Tongue River Project in the southeastern part of the state,
accompanied by my cousin Claude from Sheridan, Wyo-
ming. They were at El Rancho Gumbo for about a month
and had left early on October 15th. There had been a few
light winds during the recent days and the following morning I was awakened by higher gusts kicking up. The mountains were shrouded in a heavy cloud bank and by ten
o'clock the wind was really ripping. I could tell that something was on the way. At noon the thermometer stood at
60° above zero.

Before long I could see a distant haze across the northern
horizon and I immediately began getting things in order,
bringing in cow feed, securing the chickens, pigs, etc. But
I could find only four of the ten six-month-old pigs. When
the grain was harvested in the old way, a lot of waste remained in the fields and the livestock was turned out into
them to clean it up. The young pigs should have been in a
field close by but they were not. Suddenly at one o'clock

the 80-mile-an-hour blasts from the cloudbank in Marias Pass stopped as if some huge hand had closed the door. Within minutes a strong breeze from the north began bringing stinging pellets of snow. By sundown a blinding blizzard was in full progress and the temperature had dropped to 20° below zero. I had been unable to find the pigs, so now all I could do was wait it out, hoping they were bunched up in a safe place out of the wind. With visibility reduced to zero, there was no way to continue searching as I could not have found a box car ten feet away.

The morning of October 17th dawned bright and clear with a biting wind blowing back from the passing storm. The thermometer on the back porch now read 35° below zero. The young pigs had not returned. All of that day I searched for them in every place they might have gone but to no avail. During the days that followed, the search continued and I rode to every ranch within ten miles.

Fifty-four miles of feeder canal terminated at the top of a slope about 100 feet from the house at El Rancho Gumbo. There, it dropped over a wier into a concrete chute called the "N-O Drop". This structure, about 60-feet in length, embodied two eight-foot square stilling basins with outlet gates serving the "N" and "L" canals. At its bottom another stilling basin, between ditch banks 15-feet high, became the beginning of the "O" canal. This place usually filled with snow several feet deep and being protected from the mid-winter chinooks, remained full all winter. It never dawned on me that the pigs might be there. I kept looking for them around the straw piles somewhere. But when the snows melted in April, I found the pigs, all neatly piled up to keep warm, under ten feet of compacted snow. They were still intact, having been refrigerated all winter long.

It was a tragic loss when I needed every penny that could be scraped together.

Such was a chapter, among many others, in the saga of El Rancho Gumbo. A happening to be shrugged off with a muttered epithet, for there is no way to turn back the pages of time.

Part of our pork chop crop in 1925.

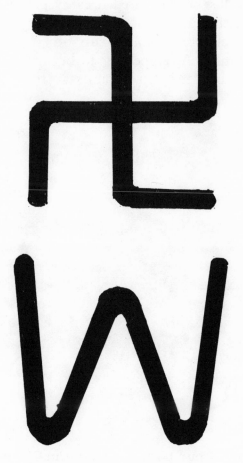

SWASTIKA W
EL RANCHO GUMBO'S LIVESTOCK BRAND

CHAPTER 24

Swastika W

I DO NOT REMEMBER the date when we obtained a live-stock brand, but it was several years before the general public had heard of Adolph Hitler. At first we thought about the "800" brand, that being the total acreage of El Rancho Gumbo owned and leased at the time. Later we decided that the Swastika would be better, being a luck symbol. Research of this character found it credited to both the ancient Chinese and the American Indian. Who-ever they were, the originators of the Swastika had threads of superstition imbedded in their religious beliefs and ap-plied them to the sign. We found the Swastika with its hooks turning to the right representing good luck; whereas, the left hand Swastika held nothing but the worst of all bad luck which could be visited upon man. Naturally we ap-plied for the right hand symbol, but to our dismay the State Recorder of Brands reversed the symbol, and we ended up with the bad luck sign. No amount of correspondence would change his mind.

At any rate, we went ahead and used the symbol as registered, and after looking back at the history of the spread it represented and later at the horrible turn of events which shook the world, I would say that it was pretty bad whichever way it turned. Our dictionary, published at a much later date, shows both types but makes no delineation in reference to luck, attributing both to good luck. It does show, however, that the left hand sign, in two variations, belongs to the Pima and Navajo Indians, while Hitler used the right hand symbol.

This may not be relative to my subject but as far as I have been able to determine, the American Indians did not apply it to their war signs in forboding manners but revered the Swastika as an omen of good. Hitler could have learned much from our native Americans and the world would have been better for it.

Our brand was on the left shoulder of both horses and cattle. It had been requested to be on the ribs of cattle, but there again, the recorder had his say.

Among old-time cowmen the Swastika was known as the Revolving L and also the Revolving 7s.

CHAPTER 25

Flats Cats

THE EARLY YEARS of El Rancho Gumbo were bad for
cats. The lure of the flats seemed to be forever taking them
into the coyote zone, for they always disappeared. Then we
acquired two half-grown brothers. Tarzan, a solid blue
Maltese, was altered, and Bluie was a tom who sported a
white vest and spats. They were as unlike as night and day.
Tarzan was a homebody, but Bluie was a wanderer whose
interests away from home prevented him from setting his
mind to developing any extraordinary traits and he barely
earned his wages.

Tarzan was an outdoor type but he also loved the house.
He slept with us and dined with us and spent many cozy
winter evenings in the Morris rocking chair, beside my
father. Whenever Dad failed to leave enough room for him,
Tarzan's grumbled complaints were sad to hear. Dad liked
to read western story magazines and kept a good supply on
hand. As he rocked and read by the big German heater, with
his Wellington pipe, he layed down a smoke screen thick
enough to asphyxiate a buffalo, but it never bothered Tarzan one bit.

Breakfast was something else again. Having never circled the globe, Tarzan was definitely not a Continental
breakfast fan. It even took some ingenuity to get him to

eat our kind. Flapjacks (pancakes), more commonly referred to as "stove lids" or "saddle blankets", were standard
items on the bachelor breakfast menu. These we made, full
skillet size, and it usually took several along with three or
four fried eggs and bacon or a pork chop or two for each
hungry hand at the table. Tarzan would have nothing but
an egg or the pork chop leavings, served on a plate on the
floor. One day Dad decided to *make* him eat a pancake but
Tarzan refused it, flat out, so Dad picked it up, broke off a
chunk and bounced it off the old cat's head. To our surprise,
Tarz' turned around and ate the cake. This was too good to
be true so the act was repeated, and from that day on Tarzan would have pancakes for breakfast every morning *if*
they were broken up and the pieces bounced off his noggin
first.

In the barnyard Tarzan was at home with the livestock,
spending chilly days on top of Dick whenever that horse
was in the stable. And whatever it is that cats do when they
dig their claws into a post, or sometimes one's best furniture,
Tarzan accomplished by digging his into Dick's hind leg. I
can't say that Dick exactly enjoyed the procedure for the
old Shire would snort fiercely as he let go with a huge hoof,
but Tarzan was never there. How he escaped annihilation
will go down in the annals of history as an unsolved mys-
tery. And strangely, Dick alone was the only "Digee" of
the shindigger cat. These were the only times Dick ever
kicked.

On at least two occasions the two cats were observed
hunting together a long way out. Each time they were
found later with a freshly butchered jackrabbit, stashed in
a manger in the stable, just minutes before a raging blizzard
struck.

The medical world had not yet decided that salt was a

major cause of hypertension and we purchased it in five pound bags made of light weight cotton material. Like the flour sacks, the empties were washed and saved for other uses. They made excellent drip bags or strainers for the home manufacturing of cottage cheese. Smearcase, as we called it, was made by setting a pan of milk on top of the warming oven of the Monarch range, leaving it there until it curdled. Then it was put into one of the salt sacks and hung on the clothesline to drip, separating the whey from the curd which was later crumbled and mixed with cream to become the finished product.

One fine spring day I inadvertently hung the cheese bag too close to the end of the line. It was, in fact, within arm's reach for my old friend Tarzan. And he was quick to seize the golden opportunity. So up the post he climbed and just as I came around the corner of the house, into view of the clothesline, I saw him hanging from the post by one hand, just like a telephone lineman, and reaching out with the other to grab the bottom of the bag. Apprehension gripped me and I shouted, surprising him and causing him to jerk, catching a claw in the bag and ripping it asunder, dropping the entire contents to the ground. Tarz took off 90-miles per hour. So much for that one, no cheese for dinner, and needless to say, me and Tarzan were not on speaking terms for the remainder of the day.

Later, choking spells began to plague Tarzan. At first we thought he had a bone stuck in his throat but then his trouble was diagnosed by a veterinarian as a goiter. Money was too scarce and in those days we did not even have medical insurance on our own hides, in fact it was unheard of, so there was no way we could spend anything on a cat. Tarzan's trouble was allowed to worsen. Early in 1935, the loyal old mouse catcher entered cat heaven and was sorely missed; especially under the soogans at the foot of the bed on frigid nights.

As for Bluie, he was not even home to attend the funeral. In fact, after having been at another ranch ten miles away, courting a maiden cat, he was never seen again. Thus ended the era of cats at El Rancho Gumbo as no replacements were ever hired on.

J. G. Wagner's government mules with scraper, excavating grade for the first road into Many Glaciers Region of Glacier National Park in 1917. This was for construction of Swiftcurrent Reservoir Dam, storage for the Milk River Irrigation Project 200 miles farther east.

The camp flunky hauling water to the mess tent on the Swiftcurrent job.

SURVEYING

CHAPTER 26

Surveying

*"I left the woods for as good a reason as
I went there. Perhaps it seemed to me that
I had several more lives to live and could
not spare any more time for that one."*
—HENRY DAVID THOREAU

AFTER I LEFT El Rancho Gumbo, it took some rattling
around before I found myself. I had grown up in agricul-
ture on a Washington fruit farm and a Montana ranch, so
I really was not prepared for anything off the land, especially working for others. After a flurry of spring farm work
for old friends I tossed my belongings into my trusty '35
Ford and headed west towards the Rockies to truck driver-
dude wrangler, hydro plant operator, hotel maintenance
plumbing and painting and beyond to damsite surveys on
the Crow Irrigation Project, and back to hotel work again.
I had begun to leave the depression behind for I was actually
getting pay checks, though some were small. And if Fisher
Flats was the womanless capital of the world, Glacier National Park was heaven on earth with its hordes of girls
among both the dudes and help. But I was still paying my
way out of El Rancho Gumbo and felt too poor to encour-
age any.

Finally I hit what to me was the Mother Lode. I landed

a job with the Seattle District Office of the U.S. Army Corps of Engineers. There was no way I was going to be incarcerated in a gas filled office or caught tossing cans of beans over a counter after all of the cool air I had enjoyed on Fisher Flats. Field surveys were the answer. On a field party, I was out in the fresh air where I could shake hands with the coyotes. This I did for 31-years (minus the war), wandering through farmers' pastures, tipping my hat to their bulls and into the hinterland, where before I got off that job, I damned near shook hands with a grizzly bear! But I didn't. I don't know where that bear is today but I know where I am and that's all that matters.

CHAPTER 27

Always Reminded

ON THE PATIO of a mountain club, our friend Myrna asked me what the years before had held. Being an old coot on the shelf ain't easy, I told her, unless one can keep up with the interesting aspects of life. I gave her a peek into my history with word pictures of a weathered log house by an alkali flat, a dozen knotheads, some cockeyed cows and a hailed out wheat field. The best steer out there, dancing in the shimmering heat waves, might bring $60 *if* Lady Luck rode in with the buyer. Knotheads were down to four bucks a head and wheat was at its all time low. It took a real thick hide, a cast iron liver and teeth that never wore down from grinding. But if a guy hung tough, better days were sure to come, and they did. Some of the better ones were hard to believe, especially when I found myself dancing with a tiny Malaysian damsel beside a moonlit pool in Singapore, for the trail of years had led outward many miles away from the bum grub batchelorhood of El Rancho Gumbo.

During the burned biscuit years on the alkali flats, when in perusing the pages of Somerset Maugham I sought refuge from the howling blizzards of Piegan country, there was no way to entertain the thought that someday I would be there. It was a far cry from El Rancho Gumbo but not for long, for after scouring the shops of Kowloon, we returned to our hotel. I turned on the T.V. only to hear a familiar voice, that of old Mr. Rifleman, himself, narrating the Yakima Indian Rodeo! Immediately the horses of El Rancho Gumbo paraded through my mind. And that was only a few days after seeing the huge bill board sign by the highway right-of-way, a jolly Japanese in feathered war bonnet and buck-skin suit, proudly advertising the Crazy Horse Bar and Lounge in downtown Tokyo.

Some months and a few 747's later found us on the mountain top in Andalusia. Inside the dimly lit structure the room was large with rows of long tables and a dance floor. As I clutched Ena's hand and pulled her through the crowd I was reminded of the 3,000 shoving, bleating sheep when I helped our neighbor on Two Medicine river at shear-ing time. Traditionally garbed Troubadours strolled among the tables, strumming their guitars, singing of everyone from conquistadores to rag time Cowboy Joe. Strobes of opportunist concessioners flashed like lightning. Photos of celebrants were everywhere. A poster, bearing the likeness of one elderly widow from a small town in Washington, showed up captioned in bold type: WANTED, DEAD or ALIVE, by the Sheriff of Virginia City. Shades of the Old West, here we were, back in the saddle again!

At Cina Cina, north of Buenos Aires, I told the old gaucho and his sons how today the horses are gone and the beautiful prairie ravaged by tractors and trucks. Their un-derstanding comment, as they nodded was: *"muy triste, muy triste"*. And to me it is indeed just that—very sad, very sad.

Coming up from B.A., our first dinner in Rio was at the popular eatery called the Rincon Gaucho which trans-lates to the Cowboy Corner, and this all boils down to just one thing:

I have to say, from Hong Kong to B.A.
There ain't no way
That I can forget
El Rancho Gumbo!

Glossary

BRONC—Any wild, unbroken or newly broken horse. Generally refers to rodeo stock, but ranch vernacular widens latitude of use to almost any horse, not an old standby.

CAYUSE—Comes from Cayuse tribe of Nez Perce Indians who were notable horsemen and original owners of blue-buttermilk horses. Incorrectly used it applies to any non-descript range bred pony or horse.

KNOTHEAD—Just another term for range horse, also called Fuzztail, Bangtail, or Broomtail.

PLUM—Slang term for "plumb", meaning all the way or completely. Not a fruit.

SALTY—Mean, ornery, wild or tricky.

SKIN—To drive a team of horses or mules.

HANDY—Chock full of bad tricks. Wild, ornery, bites, kicks, strikes.

HALTER-PULLER — An incurable psychopathic horse who pulls backwards when tethered, breaking tie rope or hitch rail. Some have demolished barns or crushed their handlers.

MULIE—Cattle term. Animal of either sex born to be hornless.

OUTLAW—Untamable or vicious horse. Usually aged or seasoned.

POLLED—Cattle term. Indicates breed of hornless cattle.

RIDGELING—A male horse born with undescended testicles. Always infertile but not impotent. Sometimes called a Ridgerunner or Original by old-timers who mangled the language. Biological: Cryptorchid. Extremely sexy, mean and hard to handle.

BUST IN TWO—To suddenly buck high with head down between the forelegs.

All that is left of El Rancho Gumbo

THIS FIRST EDITION OF
El Rancho Gumbo
HAS BEEN DESIGNED AND PRINTED BY THE
SAGEBRUSH PRESS, MORONGO VALLEY, CALIF.
THE EDITION HAS BEEN LIMITED TO
750
COPIES ONLY.

192